YOU ARE NOT BORN THAT WAY

HOMOSEXUALITY: IT'S TIME TO BREAK FREE

Shalamar Williams

Author's Tranquility Press
ATLANTA, GEORGIA

Copyright © 2023 by Shalamar Williams

All rights reserved. No part of this publication may be reproduced, distributed or transmitted in any form or by any means, including photocopying, recording, or other electronic or mechanical methods, without the prior written permission of the publisher, except in the case of brief quotations embodied in critical reviews and certain other noncommercial uses permitted by copyright law. For permission requests, write to the publisher, addressed "Attention: Permissions Coordinator," at the address below.

Shalamar Williams/Author's Tranquility Press
3800 Camp Creek Pkwy SW Bldg. 1400-116 #1255
Atlanta, GA 30331, USA
www.authorstranquilitypress.com

Ordering Information:
Quantity sales. Special discounts are available on quantity purchases by corporations, associations, and others. For details, contact the "Special Sales Department" at the address above.

You Are Not Born That Way/Shalamar Williams
Paperback: 978-1-962859-29-5
eBook: 978-1-962859-30-1

Prayer

LORD, WE NEED YOU TO HELP OUR WORLD. HELP YOUR PEOPLE SO THEY WILL SEE THE TRUE LIGHT WHICH IS YOU. LORD, EVEN THOUGH WE TEACH YOUR WORD AND WE TEACH AGAINST SIN, WE STILL NEED YOUR HELP LORD. HEAL YOUR PEOPLE LORD, THANK YOU FOR BRINGING ME OUT AND SETTING ME FREE OF THIS HOMOSEXUALITY LIFESTYLE, AND THE ANOINTING THAT YOU HAVE GIVEN ME. NOW LORD, I ASK THAT YOU SET SOULS FREE OF THIS LIFESTYLE AND SHOW THEM THAT YOU ARE REAL AND LIFE DOESN'T HAVE TO BE LIVED IN SIN, SHOW THEM THAT YOU MADE MAN FOR WOMAN AND WOMAN FOR MAN. LORD, HELP PEOPLE TO UNDERSTAND THIS BOOK THAT I'M WRITING AND HELP THIS BOOK TO TOUCH THE HEARTS OF YOUR PEOPLE. THESE THINGS I ASK IN YOUR SON JESUS NAME...

AMEN.

Contents

Chapter One 6

Chapter Two 15

Chapter Three 22

Chapter Four 29

Chapter Five 34

Chapter Six 38

Chapter One

Trust and understand that this homosexual life that people want to live is nothing but the devil, God made man for woman and woman for man, we shall understand that the bible doesn't lie, and we must live in spirit and in truth. **1 Corinthians 11:9 KJV** tells us that: *Neither was the man created for the woman, but the woman for the man.* So, if the bible tells us that the man wasn't created for woman, but the woman was created for man, how is it that we think it's okay for two women to lay together and two men to lay together? It doesn't matter what people here on earth say it's okay to do because man are flesh, man are not God that's why it's always a good thing to study the word of God for yourself. Our leaders of this world must take a stand for holiness how can the leaders of this world overrule God and say it's okay for two of the same sex to be together when God says it's not.

It's time to break free of this strong hole that the devil has on the life of homosexuality. You must break free in Jesus name, and I am a living witness that the chain can be broken. You just have to give it to Jesus, you are not born that way so stop allowing the devil to tell you that you are. God has a plan for everyone's life, God knew what he wanted you to do before you became flesh. You were a spirit before you became flesh, God knew that some would fall and some would go astray, but understand that all power is in the hands of Jesus where he can turn life around for you. A lot of times it's not God's will for us to do things that we do in this life, but it's we, ourselves that move in the wrong direction and we give the devil power over our lives. Don't allow the devil to tell you that you were born that way because you weren't born that way, because God created you and we all know that God didn't send us into his world gay.

I have lived that life and it wasn't for me. Yes, I thought that I was in love with that woman, and yes I thought I wanted to marry a woman. But when Jesus got a hold on me, my life changed when Jesus started speaking to me. I didn't have to fight the devil because that one touch from Jesus changed my life, HALLELUJAH! My life was changed and I was set free of that lifestyle and I have been running for Jesus ever since. It's okay to walk away from everything because I'm a witness of Jesus who will bless you double, just because you gave up the world to follow him.

I was brought up in church and I knew right from wrong, I knew Jesus and I knew about sin but what did I do, I ran away from God over into the devil's hands. But God didn't stop loving me, God still kept his hands on me and when I think about that part it gives me joy in my heart, I don't care what people say. Jesus will always be that faithful one, the one that you can put all your trust in. When I was in sin, it felt good at the time, but I always had that conviction in my heart because I knew that way of living was wrong. At the time I didn't care because I was so caught up in the world and the devil was making me feel really good. But when the devil thought I have her now she is hail bound things started to go wrong no matter where turned in life, but in this book, I'm going to give you the word of God and how life should be lived as man and woman, so I pray that the words that I speak will help somebody and blessed somebody's heart that want to step out of this lifestyle and give their life to God because living a gay lifestyle is part of the devil and it is sin and you must come out and allow God to set your souls free. God is willing to help you. You have to take the first step and God will lead and guide you from there. Trust and believe the words that I say Jesus will help you through this.

Leviticus 18:22 KJV BIBLE

Thou shalt not lie with mankind, as with womankind:
it is abomination.

Homosexuality, we must obey the word of God even if we don't like what the bible tells us, but understand living the way the bible tells us to live and obeying the word of God. Living and walking in the word of God is what's going to get us into the kingdom of heaven, living this homosexual life will not get you into the kingdom of heaven. We must obey God, and I understand that this world is saying that it's okay to be this way but it's not. So what this bible verse tells me is laying with mankind and laying with womankind is an abomination and I will not make it into the kingdom of heaven when Jesus parts the sky. Now you may choose to live any way you choose but ask yourself, is living a gay lifestyle worth me going to hell and burning to eternity? I can tell you right now that it's not worth it, you'll be losing your life because in hell there is no life, but in heaven you will live forever with Jesus. Don't think that people didn't live this lifestyle before our time, if they didn't, then it wouldn't be in the Book of Life. But God sees all and God knows all whatever is done. God made a woman from a man's rib for a woman to be a help mate to man, not for a woman to act like a man and lay with another woman and it's the same way for man. God made you in his image for you to lead not for you to follow. Eva allowed the devil to use her and

Adam felt weak and allowed his wife to convince him to eat from the tree. If this wouldn't have happened they would not have known sin, the world would have been a better place. But when they eat from the tree which was wicked, then their eyes were opened and God found them naked in the garden, they tried to hide from God but God already knew what they had done.

Just because Adam and Eva didn't get it right, that doesn't mean that the world have to live in sin, they had to leave their home because they disobeyed God and this is what will happen when you disobey God and don't live the way he has called for us to live. We go through things in life that we shouldn't, yet because we don't obey God, he allows things to happen in our lives. You must break free of this sin and give your life to God, your first love and your last love Jesus Christ. I'm not saying that God doesn't care about you because you are in sin, it's because God loves us all, but God did say that sin will send us to hell and there is no life in hell.

We all have a purpose in this life, but it's up to us to come to Jesus and find out what's our purpose why we are here. Because God has a purpose for your life and God wants to use you in this life to spread his word and tell of his goodness. When God brought me out of sin, I knew that God had a plan for my life. I just had to give my all to God and I didn't know that I would be teaching the word of God, but he called me to teach. I didn't know I was called to lay hands on the sick and they would be healed but God had a plan for my life that I couldn't see at the time I was in sin. But when I came out of sin God poured out in my life and on my life, Jesus is real I don't care who believes it or not, but Jesus is real and I know for myself that Jesus can turn any dead situation into a living situation and I thank God because I have a purpose in this life and I have a purpose within my soul and that purpose is Jesus the Holy Ghost because when purpose starts moving inside of me, I give God all the praise because if it had not been for Jesus, I know for sure that I would be dead and gone, but Jesus spoke and said: "I see the sin you are in, I see your heart, I see all the wrong that you have done, but you have a purpose and I'm going to bring you out and you will tell of my goodness what a mighty God will serve". Jesus is life and we must live in the will of God because, without Jesus, there would be no life. Jesus is the reason that this world is not just out of control, yet even though things are happening in this world, it will not be out of control because if it was Jesus would have already come and taken the righteous ones out of here, so thank God that he still has his hands on this world.

What if God treated us like we treated him, some people think that there is no God, it's just a higher power. But understand that God is the higher power, he gives life and he takes life away, God has the power to raise the dead and some think that there is no God. Come out of sin because on that day when Jesus make his return what will you say when he part the sky? You don't want Jesus to come back and you don't know him and he don't know you because the words you will hear Jesus say is, "I don't know you depart from me, you don't want to hear Jesus say those words when he part the sky this is the reason why I teach the word of God like I do because people need to know about God and they need to know what the bible say about sin, some people in my family treat me like an outsider because I do what God has called me to do and that's teach on sin and tell his people that if you don't come out of sin, in hell you shall be and I'm fine with people and family acting the way they act. I pray for them and I keep doing the will of God because God has called me to teach I know it's sad for the family to be that way but they loved me when I was in sin, but as soon as God saved me and called me to teach his word everybody started calling the pastor talking about you need to set Shalamar down because they don't like truth and the devil can't stand the light that Jesus puts over my life the devil will never like light. Sin is sin and we must come out and come to Jesus because Jesus is the way the truth and the light and people can't stand the truth.

But it's crazy how when people need you to pray in a life-or-death situation because they love you. Then one thing I have learned is you have to pray for them because God tells us to pray even though sometimes is hard, but I must obey and do the will of God like he has called me to do. I will never in life again allow sin to come into my life and separate me from my Lord and Savior because I know who has my back, Jesus. When you have Jesus on your side you can make it, you can keep walking because Jesus is walking with you, you just have to come out of sin and give your life to God and allow Jesus to be everything you need. Laying with another woman can't give you what you need and laying with another man can't give you what you need. Give up that part in your life, walk away from it and run to Jesus because Jesus can and he will fix everything in you that needs to be fixed.

I know a lot of people have ran to that lifestyle because I was hurt. I wasn't that child who was the favorite, I saw it and I felt it as well as other people and God saw that part broke me down in life, but look at my life now, God took all that pain and he turned it into Holy Ghost power and some are wishing that they were where I am now in life. God brought me out of sin saved me gave me a husband using me to teach his word. I may not have been the favorite, but I was chosen by God. That alone gives me joy in my heart. So don't allow the pain from your past to keep you in sin. Fight for the good and come out because God has a lot of work for you to do, God will deal with the ones that didn't treat you right. Just come out of sin and give your life to him. It doesn't matter what the world sees, you ask yourself what do God see me as? Don't allow the devil to rob you of the power that God has given you. To come out of sin, God has given you the power of prayer. Ask anything in his name and it shall be done. Same sex should not lay with one another doing sexual things because it's a disgrace in the eyesight of God and we are doing something that God tells us not to do. The devil wants people to believe that this is right and that you still can enter into heaven but it isn't true, the devil is a liar and the devil does things to conceive our minds and we think things that we do are right but what will God say and what has God already said about it so who will you believe, God or Satan.

1 Corinthians 2:9 KJV Bible

It says, But as it is written, eyes hath not seen, nor ears heard, neither have entered into the heart of man, the things which God hath prepared for them that love him.

This bible verse can be used for many examples. Man, only if you knew what woman God has prepared for you and the happiness that came with that woman, would you still look to another man to Satisfy your needs? Woman, if you knew what man God has prepared for you and the happiness that came with that man, would you still look to another woman to Satisfy your needs? I don't think you would. Why? because a lot people that has chosen this homosexual lifestyle haven't given a woman or a man time to come into their life and be what God has placed them in your life to be. I can testify of this just because of one man or woman broke your heart doesn't mean all man and woman are the same that person just wasn't for you but we can't run out and get with the same sex and think this is what God has for my life because it's not what

God has for your life. I am guilty that a man broke my heart and that's why I ran to a woman because of hurt. I didn't allow God to fix me back up I ran to a woman/women because it made me feel happy not knowing that it was the devil deceiving me and robbing me of my happiness. But understand that we must run to Jesus, the one where our happiness starts, because it doesn't start with a woman being with another woman and a man being with another man, it's a sin in the eyesight of God, and if we don't come out, in hell we will lift our eyes. You must come out and allow God to fix you. God wants to save you. If God didn't want to save you, then God wouldn't be sending the word, "Come out of sin, and homosexuality isn't the only sin." God is saying that come out because there is a lot of sin. People must come out.

I am talking to the homosexuality community because I once lived this lifestyle and this is what God has given me to deal with and talk about because I know the fight that the homosexuality community has to deal with when you don't have to choose this life. People are been killed just because they choose to live in homosexuality and it's not right for you to stay there in that situation and allow the devil to steal your life from you, God wants to give you life where you can live it more abundantly. So listen to the words that I speak which is through Jesus Christ, come out of sin because you were not born that way.

Parents, what do you stand for if we can't tell our children the truth? Some parents accept what their children want, but as parents, we must tell our children that God didn't bring them into this world to be gay, God brought you into this world to do work for him. Stop allowing your children to tell you that they are gay and tell your children what God says, they are man and woman and God created woman for man and man for woman. It's our job as parents to pray with our children, I don't care how old they are, pray with them and pray for them. Don't accept what the devil allows, but accept what God allows and that's the truth. Give your children the truth and love your children. I have to speak what God has laid on me, we can't control sickness like aids that come with this lifestyle but we can control how far we allow the devil to take us the devil does what we allow him to do, prayer is what keeps the devil away from our home and our children, pray because God hears your prayer.

Come out of sin and be made over be washed in the blood of Jesus, it's sick to me the way the news is saying that leaders want to allow children under age to get a sex change, that is not what God has called you to be. I'm asking every parent when it comes to the devil who is allowing children under age to have a sex change to rethink and pray about it, because God gave you that son and that daughter to be some woman's husband to be some man's wife, not to be made into something that they are not. God told Adam and Eve in **Genesis 1:28 KJV**, *to be fruitful, and multiply, and replenish the earth*. Man can't have children even with a sex change so don't allow the devil to make you into something that God didn't.

Chapter Two

Resources to fight

God has given us the resources that we need to live life in joy and in peace, but we must live life the way the bible tells us to live life. I haven't been always saved and I have lived that sinful life. I have lived life with the devil and I thought I was living my best life, but when I came into contact with Jesus, I found my best life and Jesus has been giving me everything I need to keep fighting for him. It took a lot of prayer to get to this point where I am now in life it didn't happen overnight but I made it through. Yes the devil has tried to tempt me at times but I didn't give up on God because I knew that God wouldn't give up on me, I made it through hard times when the devil was telling me to go back to that woman. I had to tell that devil that he was a liar because that's not why God brought me into this world to lay with same-sex womankind, I had to remember what Jesus said in **John chapter 10:11**, *I am the good shepherd: the good shepherd giveth his life for the sheep.* So if God which is the good shepherd gives life for me, why can't I give my life back to him? I didn't want the pain of that lifestyle anymore I wanted to be happy with Jesus, because if I choose to follow my flesh, I would be hell-bound, and I knew that it was God who called me to teach because amid the devil talking to me, trying to get me to return to that homosexual lifestyle, I could still hear Jesus speaking giving me a word to speak to overcome my flesh. Jesus was telling me now that I am the beginning in the end, and the only way to have life is through him. So this is why I can tell anybody you can come out of that homosexual lifestyle and you can beat your strongholds that the devil tries to use to hold you back from making it to your destiny which is Jesus Christ.

Every time I think about where God has brought me from, I get happy because I have been through some things in life and I know Jesus is the reason why I was able to walk away from it. I still have people who hold my past lifestyle over my head but it's okay with me because all it's doing is making me praise God even harder, this is how you win anytime the devil brings your past. Don't allow it to make you feel bad and allow it to make you. Praise God because not only you don't forget where God has brought you from, but the devil wants you to forget that God has come to hell and took what belongs to him. So the devil can only take what we allow him to take, but I dare you to come out of sin and take your life back and put it in the hands of the highest Jesus Christ, and watch and see what God does in your life, I'm a witness if you take one step to God and God will take two steps and set you in a place of peace because, in God, there is peace.

Don't think that I'm not praying for the world to come out of sin because there's a lot of sin in this world but what I can testify to is living in a homosexual lifestyle because this was my life and I know how hard the devil works in this lifestyle because the devil knows that everyone wants to be loved but I have to tell you that a homosexual lifestyle that life isn't love, Jesus loves you the devil just have you where he wants you because that devil is saying I got them I won't be the only one in hail. But what we must understand is if Jesus went to hail and took the keys and Jesus said I have the keys to life or death then that should tell you that Jesus paid for our sins and we don't have to choose hail we can choose life and live and not die because hail is death and Jesus is life and light. Darkness can't comprehend light darkness know Jesus not so repent for your wicked ways we must choose Jesus and not the world because the world love it's own. It tell us in the bible if we Love Jesus we will keep his commandments, so we must obey God's will and keep all his commandments there is no way that we should be able to marry woman and woman and man and man but in some places in this world the law is allowing it to happen. We must live by the law of God and do as we should do as God children, God will bless you if you live right God will send that right man or woman in your life but first we have to let go of the sin that the devil has in the world. God is already blessing you by waking you up everyday so that alone should tell you that God loves you and he is giving you a chance to get it right. And we all know that Jesus is real but I am praying for the world and for the one's that say they don't know Jesus which this is the time that we should want to know him because we are living in the last times just look at the world and how things are going on and how they are changing laws to make the homosexual feel good about a sinful lifestyle. But we look at life and do things just because it seems fun well there's nothing fun about being gay it's sin, I thank God I can look at that devil and say pass me by and I can look up towards heaven and say Jesus don't pass me by because I'm yours Jesus here I am do what you want to do in my life because if it had not been for you I wouldn't have life but we are so stuck on fun and sin that we can't see the big picture and that's Jesus, fun things can't save you but God can material things money homes can't keep you happy but Jesus can laying with another man can't keep you happy or laying with another woman can't keep you happy but Jesus can why because Jesus is were happiness starts my bible tells me John 3:16 for God so love the world that he gave in only begotten son, that whosoever believeth in him should not perish but have everlasting life. This is what we shall believe the word of God. Give your life to God today come to your first love and your last love come and fight the good fight because you are not getting by living in sin you are not getting by dealing with sin we can't be evil does you must walk away from something that God didn't create for you to deal with. Don't think that God doesn't see all things don't think that God don't hear all things God sees the heart and I know that there are some people that want to come out of sin but the devil have a strong whole on their life but I pled the blood of Jesus over your life that you will break free.

Deuteronomy 7:9 KJV

Know therefore that the Lord your God is God; he is the faithful God, keeping his covenant of love to a thousand generations of those who love him and keep his commandments.

We must know that God is the faithful God the only God, God is faithful even when we are not, been faithful to God means keeping his commandments and standing in Holiness, I'm trying to understand why are people so faithful to sin and so faithful to man and woman but we can't be faithful to God and the will of God. 1 John 1:9 KJV tell us If we confess our sins, he is faithful and just to forgive us our sins, and to cleanse us from all unrighteousness. See when we confess we are telling God I need your help we are telling God yes I am a sinner and when we confess our sins this is when God will come in our heart and clean us and heal us but some people will reject God when he call their name because of sin has them feeling like this is the life for them, but the key to been delivered is to call on the name of Jesus in Jesus name there is power healing power and break through power see people know the name of Jesus but are you really calling on his name because if you really just start calling on the name of Jesus he will show up that's how I got my healing that's how I made it through calling on the name of Jesus. Jesus is willing to do a work in us I am asking someone to allow Jesus to set your soul free because Jesus can and he will bring you out of darkness into the light, I say all the time it's like Holy Ghost firer shut up in my bones because I know what Jesus has done in my life, will you allow him to work in your life? You will not be able to call on the name of Jesus without something moving on the inside get your healing just call on the name of Jesus I don't care because you are in sin call on the name of Jesus because Jesus will show up sin will be removed you can come out of sin calling on the name of Jesus. Understand that powerful is our God I have never seen the righteous forsaken nor his seed begging bread come and taste and see that the Lord is good in all his ways.

Not long ago, I was asleep and it was about three in the morning. God came into my bedroom and allowed me to spell the fragrance of God, I opened my eyes because this was a fragrance that I never smelled before and not only was it in my nose, it was in my mouth and it tasted so good. So I message my Godfather evangelist Robert Shepherd and told him what I was smelling and he began to tell me about the fragrance of God, I couldn't do anything but cry and thanking God telling him Lord you love me this much, even my past couldn't stop God from loving me, my sins couldn't stop God from loving me. This is why I say no matter what you do in life, make sure you come back to your first love, I didn't understand how God could take my dirty soul and clean me up and use me to tell about his goodness, but he did and I thank him everyday of my life because God has used me to lay hands on the sick and they were healed, what I am telling you is God get the glory out of my life because my life belongs to him, he is my father, the one who is using me to talk to the homosexuality and let them know if he brought me out of this lifestyle he can bring you out and use you like he is using me. I give all praise to God because he is worried of my praise.

If you knew the man that I'm talking about and the works that he has done in my life knowing that he can do the same for you, you would be praising God sin you will walk away from and obey, God doesn't allow the devil to tell you that God can't use you, because God can and God will use you. Come out of sin and tell that devil that he is a liar. Come and try Jesus the man that I speak highly of and I promise you will be singing the same song that I am singing, Repent and come out of sin. Victory isn't in sin, victory is in Jesus. If sin has so much victory, Why are you sad? Why are you depressed? Why can't you smile? You are not happy in sin, victory, joy, peace, and life are in Christ Jesus. I know what sin will have you looking like and feeling like I was mad all the time I had an attitude all the time. I have been there in sin, but the difference is, that God saved me and delivered me. So there is no victory in sin, just come to Jesus, come to Jesus and give your life to him. Give God a true yes and stand firm and wait for God to do work in you. Obeying the bible is where your victory comes from, make up your mind to live for Jesus, and tell God I trust you, Lord I believe in your word, I know that you are God I see that you are God.

1 John 2, KJV it says,

and hereby we do know that we know him, if we keep his commandments, He that saith, I know him and keepeth not his commandments is a liar, and the truth is not in him.

Come out of sin and keep God's commandments. Don't you know if we keep God's commandments, God will keep us. God will keep us from falling because when you have the Holy Ghost, that means you have an advocate with the Father Jesus Christ, the righteous one the Holy One Jesus Christ, we must Praise the name of Jesus because he is good in all his ways. This is why we have to come out of sin because God is good to us, it's us that's not good to God. Come out of sin and allow God to do his job. Seek the Lord, cry out for the Lord, he will hear your cry. Oh my God, as I sit here writing, I feel the power of the Holy Ghost because God did it for me God save my dirty soul and he filled me with the Holy Ghost when I think. See, I don't need the devil to think for me, it's when I think about the goodness of God that my soul cries out a HALLELUJAH!, because hallelujah is the highest. Praise that we can give God, the chains have been broken and I am free and I can tell someone now who is reading and will read this book that God will break the chains that has you tried down and Jesus is going to raise up a stander against that devil. When you call on the name of Jesus, yes Lord break every chain and set your people free Hallelujah Jesus is life.

Chapter Three

Hold on and Let Go

If we love God we will keep his commandments, I love the saying *hold on and let go*, because this is something that the older women would tell you at the altar. Hold on and let go and what they were saying was you have to let go of sin and you have to hold on to God. Holding on to God is your life, holding on to the devil is death because there is no life in sin, give everything that's wrong on the inside of you to Jesus because God will carry your load. Nothing is too hard for God so hold on and let go.

Leviticus 11:44-45 KJV says...

44: For I am the Lord your God: ye shall therefore sanctify yourselves, and ye shall be holy; for I am holy; neither shall ye defile yourselves with any manner of creeping thing that creepeth upon the earth.

45: For I am the Lord that bringeth you up out of the land of Egypt, to be your God: ye shall therefore be holy, for I am holy.

God Holy In the past, God Holy in the present and God Holy in the future, who was and is and is to come this is why I cry Holy because my mind is made up and this is what we have to have is a made up mind to come out of sin and serve the Lord thy God. Jesus said I am that I am past, present and the future, I see part of my past was sin but I knew when God stepped in, my past wouldn't control my future even though people would throw my past in my face, because I was looking to the hills for which cometh my help, this is why I cry Holy. Because of the way, God brought me out of sin some of my family didn't like it but he brought me out of sin and put me right back in the midst of my family and the devil knew that my life had changed and God was using me for his glory and I was fine with the devil doing his job, but I wasn't okay because it was some of my family that the devil was using but I took what God gave me which is the power of the Holy Ghost to keep moving and because of God I still cry Holy to this day. I didn't allow this to stop me, I kept crying out to God, I kept praying and looking to Jesus, the author and finisher of my faith shame on the devil, not me shame on the devil because I made it out that homosexual lifestyle with Jesus and I am free this is why I cry Holy. If they take the word away, I will still cry Holy because the word of Jesus is in my heart, I thank God that my past is dead and gone and I'm living in the presence of Holiness and I will live in the future of holiness, it doesn't matter my mind is made up will you make up your mind today? Will you tell that devil that his time is up? And run to Jesus so everything about you can be Holy your walk your talk your hands your feet your tongue will you walk out of sin today and give your life to Jesus? I have asked God to shape me the way that he wants me to be shape me Lord were I would stand for you and don't take down because the devil has got nervous because he knows that his little kingdom is about to go down in flames because I will stand with the power that God has giving me and be lead by Jesus to help souls come out of sin and be set free and come back to their first love Jesus Christ. Come out of sin because Jesus is waiting there is no shame in been saved there is no shame in calling on the name of Jesus don't allow the devil to keep you vexed irritated and annoyed one thing that I do know is you don't want God to get irritated with you so now is the time to come out of sin and cry Holy Lord make me over for give me of my sin. Pray this prayer with me: Lord I need you help me there is no way I can make it out in this world without you forgive me of my sins come into my life and make me whole Lord I confess with my mouth that you are Lord and you died for my sin I believe in my heart that you went to the cross for me where I would have life with you Amen. Now you are just as saved as anyone else now walk the walk and talk the talk live your life upright in Jesus Christ and you shall see for yourself that God is good in all his ways. Matthew 11:28-30 KJV Come unto me all ye that labour and are heavy laden, and I will give you rest. Take my yoke upon you, and learn of me for I am meek and lowly in heart and ye shall find rest unto your souls for my yoke is easy and my burden is light.

Come out and learn of the Lord nothing is to hard for God His yoke is easy and his burdens are light so why should you stay in sin If God is telling you that his yoke is easy and his burdens are light, that's just enough for me to trust God and cry Holy Lord the devil can't stop your burdens the devil can't give you peace the devil can't deliver you but I know of a man that can turn water into wine I know a man that can make the blind see I know a man that can raise the dead I know a man that can put bones back together I know a man who can touch you and change your mind I know a man who can just blow and walls start to come down I know a man that can make the trees praise him this is why I cry Holy Lord. My praise is what keeps me from going back into sin because if our praise didn't help us then flesh will kill us God is a keeper we just have to want to be kept we have to stay away from the things and people that will tempt you to go back into sin we must stay away from it.

2 Corinthians 6:14

Be ye not unequally yoked together with unbelievers for what fellowship hath righteousness with unrighteousness and what communion hath light with darkness.

Paul made the word clear when he was telling them to open their hearts again to Jesus, I love how Paul gave a direct command that believers in Christ is not to be yoked with unbelievers There is no way you got the Holy Ghost and you say that God has brought you out of sin and you are still hanging with your unbeliever friends how can two walk together except they agree. When I got saved I couldn't continue to walk with the one's I walked with because I would be a lair and that's giving someone false doctrine I had to let go everything that was connected to that homosexual lifestyle because I knew it wouldn't be easy if I stayed around that lifestyle I had to run away from it and keep my eyes on Jesus so no there is no way you can still walk with the devil and say that I have been delivered the devil is a lair don't allow the devil to trap you like that you must break free from it all understand that temptation is real and this is what the devil use against us temptation because the devil know that it is wrong so we must know the difference between fidelity and infidelity the devil temped God so who are we but we have the power to tell the devil what God told the devil get the behind me Satan and keep pressing towards the mark for the prize of the high calling of God in Jesus Christ, keep pushing keep walking in the light of Jesus Christ and he will help you to over come all temptation that's in the world.

I have to also talk about men and women that are gay and they are hiding it undercover. **Proverbs 28:13 KJV** tells us, *He that covereth his sin shall not prosper but who so confesseth and forsaketh them shall have mercy.* You shouldn't cover your sin and think you have it alright with Jesus this may ruffle some feathers. I have to speak what God has giving me to speak, there are some married men and women that have husbands and wives and you are undercover and some are going to church every Sunday, like you are not doing anything wrong and you want your spouse to believe that you are faithful and Holy Ghost filled shame on you, go and check your oil. You don't serve the God that I serve, I must give you the truth because it's so many people out in the world who are so educated in books but not educated in Jesus. These people tell you that it is right but God said it is wrong, read it for yourself it's in the bible.

How can you love your spouse but lay with another woman or lay with another man and you are married something isn't right this is living in darkness confess your wrongs confess your sin and come out of darkness and come to Jesus who is light. If you are saved, you shouldn't have to be in darkness. You shouldn't be angry all the time at your spouse and they think it's something wrong with them. No, it something wrong with you, come out of sin, you go home late and leave home early because you don't want that man or that woman, but you don't want the world to know that you are gay so you stay there to make your spouse stuff with your problem. This is not of God but if you confess your sin, Jesus is faithful and he will forgive you of your sins. How can you get to heaven in sin, there is no way you can you have to be clean on the inside. God doesn't care what the outside looks like, God cares about what the inside of us looks like.

You get mad when people are teaching on sin and you get happy when someone says heaven, but what I will tell you is you can kiss heaven goodbye when Jesus Returns, and you, in your sins in hell, you will lift your eyes and there is no life in hell. How can you talk about heaven, and you in your sins, this is the part that makes me sick to my stomach. Do some Pastors are undercover and you are in the pull pit? Teaching this is what some people confuse with Pastors, you are in the pull pit undercover and you are teaching a lie and people are following in it.

1 John 4 in KJV

Beloved, believe not every spirit but try the spirits whether they are of God: because many false prophets are gone out into the world.

The only way we can try the spirits and know if it is of God, we have to have the spirit of God in us to be able to pinpoint false teaching and false prophets, you can't allow everybody to teach you, make sure that you are under a pastor that's going to give you the truth. If a pastor can't teach on sin but full of prosperity messages, you need to run away because if you are living right, God is going to bless you with all you need. So you don't need someone telling you prosperity things all the time because if your soul is right, God is going to take good care of you. **Deuteronomy 28 KJV** tell us *The Lord your God will bless you in the land he is giving you. The Lord will establish you as his holy people, as he promised you on earth.* If you keep the commands of the Lord your God and walk in his ways, then all the people on earth will see that you are called by the name of the Lord, and they will fear you. So why do I need someone every Sunday teaching prosperity messages to me and when God has already promised in the book of Deuteronomy chapter 28. I have been called by the name of the Lord and I will walk in the path that Jesus has given me I am blessed I don't need anyone to prophesy prosperity to me because I walk in the light of Jesus Christ. I can tell God what he promised me, because if Jesus said it that settles it. I want to bless someone's soul with truth I have to help God and people see the truth about life and how life should be lived life has to be lived through Jesus Christ life is Jesus and death is the devil you have to come out of sin to be able to have life and live it as Jesus has instructed us to Amen.

Chapter Four

Pharaoh, Let My People Go

Exodus 9:1 KJV

Then the Lord said unto Moses, Go in unto Pharaoh, and tell him. Thus saith the Lord God of the Hebrews, Let my people go, that they may serve me.

I have to come up against the devil and tell him to let God's people go because all nations belong to God. All humans belong to God we are made in the image of God and he died for us so that we didn't have to be trapped by Pharaoh. I am calling for homosexuality to come out of sin and take a hand with me up against the devil. I once was living a homosexual lifestyle, I came out with Jesus on my side and God has done a work in me. I am saved, sanctified and filled with the Holy Ghost and I have the power that Jesus has given me when he filled me with the Holy Ghost to speak to dry bones.

Come out and Join me on the side of Jesus because there is hope peace love and joy. God is a great God, he understands you, he understands your pain and God is waiting to hear your call. God is waiting for you to make that one step, Come out of sin laying with mankind or womankind, this isn't of God. This lifestyle isn't right and if you don't come out there, there is no way you will see Jesus. I know people are telling you to live your life but God is saying come out of that homosexual life because it's of the devil, This just didn't start in our time, this was going on before the time and God wasn't pleased with it. Now, we must break free and be healed in the name of Jesus Christ. He is our keeper, he has kept me so I know he will keep you, lean on Jesus. **Proverbs KJV** it says *Trust in the Lord with all thine heart and lean not unto thine own understanding*. People in sin don't trust the Lord but it goes both ways. People living in sin, God can't trust you but I hear people say *"I trust in the Lord"*. When they know they are in sin, my thing is how can you trust in the Lord and you want to live by his law but you can put your trust in man, that means you know good this is and how the devil has your mind. Pharaoh, let God's people go devil, the world has a clear understanding of sin and the world trusts in you and not God but Pharaoh. You must let God's people go Pharaoh who did you go and die for. People put their trust in you. Shame on you that you wanted to be God and rule over God and got kicked out of heaven into the pit of hell. Now you want the world to believe that it's okay to be in sin, you want people to believe that you are their saver, I rebuke you in the **MIGHTY NAME OF JESUS!** Your time is running out Pharaoh, for I know deep down in my soul that God is good and he will help flesh come out of sin.

Understand when you lean or lay on Jesus, he has to help you because he's a man that who shall not lie, I know what I am saying is right because I was once in sin and that lifestyle is trash compared to Jesus that's who feels good. Jesus, try him and come out of sin, Jesus will help you he will heal you. He will cover you, just lean on Jesus, don't think that God doesn't understand, he knows all things. Try him and see, start calling on the name of Jesus, and tell that devil, *"I take a stand against you and I am going back to my first love who is Jesus Christ."* Tell that devil that you have been down for too long and you have to go and do what God has put you here to do no more of mankind and no more of womankind. I have been unhappy for a long time, now but I know with Jesus. I have life and I will be free of all my sins speak over yourself in the name of Jesus, because I am asking God that whoever picks up this book and reads it, will be set free and made whole by the power of the Holy Ghost and they shall see all things that you have for them in this life.

Lord, bless your people to see the light and not the darkness. Lord, call their name where they will come to you and obey you and your word that they may do your will, in Jesus name, Amen.

Don't allow the devil to steal from your life that Jesus has given you to live free and in happiness. Look to Jesus for whatever you need because God will get the glory out of your life, I thank God for my life because I have been blessed in so many ways, just for walking out of sin and looking to Jesus, the author and finisher of my faith, Jesus is able if God lead the children of Israel. I know that God will lead you when you choose to come out of sin and give your life to him walk through the gate to Jesus who is truth and I promise you that you will rise because you have made up in your mind that you are coming out and giving your life to Jesus.

Matthew 7:13-14 KJV tells us to...

13: Enter ye in at the strait gate: for wide is the gate, and broad is the way, that leadeth to destruction, and many there be which go in thereat.

14: Because strait is the gate, and narrow is the way, which leadeth unto life, and few there be that find it.

You Are Not Born Thay Way

The Strait Gate is the Holy Gate, the Strait Gate is the upright gate and there is no sin. You have to come out of sin in order to walk through this strait gate and let go of homosexuality because it's not the strait gate, it's the gate of destruction. You must come out of this sinful lifestyle it's not of God, he made man for woman and woman for man that's just how it is, God is saying come out and come to him. I know people are asking whom she thinks she is talking about sin, she was gay so now she's trying to tell us to come out. You are right, "was gay" is the key word which is past tense and I'm not the one who is saying come out of sin, Jesus is saying come out of sin, he's just using me to show the devil he has no power, because whatever God touch, he can clean and shape it to what he want it to be. And because God has laid his hands on me and shaped me and molded me into what he wants me to be. That's why I can stand and tell you to come out because God has given me the power to rise and overcome the sin that I was in. People didn't expect me to come out of that lifestyle but God made that devil out of a lie because I have been washed by the blood of Jesus.

I know your pain for the ones who are fighting to come out, but Jesus can turn your pain into power, I can relate to you. That's why God is using me because I know what it takes to come out of sin and be free. I have cried just like you, that's why I can tell you God will give you the power to overcome the devil, just tell God yes to his will, yes to his way, yes I will go and yes I will stand still in your will. Stop saying yes to the devil and say yes to God by coming out of sin. Ask yourself, is going to hell worth living in sin? Come out of sin woman, leave that woman, and come to God. Man, leave that man and come to God, because he will supply all your needs according to his riches and glory by Christ Jesus. Your prayer of faith shall save you and set you free and understand that there is no want in Jesus and allow God to give you peace. God tells us his peace, he leaves with us, and his peace he gives unto us not as the world gives, trust God he's a man who can't lie.

I remember when that woman told me that I couldn't make it without her, where is that devil now? because I would love for her to see me living in the will of God because God has given me everything even his peace. Will someone come out of sin and see for themselves that the Lord is good and his mercy is forever? I thank God that his mercy kept me when I was living in sin mercy saved me and showed me another life and I thank God because I believe what Jesus has to say about me not the devil. I shall live and not die and I'm telling you the same you shall live and not die if you come out of sin. You can come out and put your trust in God, not man or woman but God. Allow God to be your rock and stop taking gifts from the devil. Come and receive the gift of life in Jesus Christ because you don't want to hear Jesus say *'I never knew you, depart from me'*, so you shall come out of sin and receive the gift of the Holy Ghost, Jesus is real, try him, Jesus loves you, try him, when you call on Jesus he will answer your call, he did it for me and I know that Jesus will do it for you because Jesus has no respectable person. This is why we need preachers to preach the truth which is Holiness or Hail tell the truth to help God's people come out of sin and if preachers can't tell God's people the truth, they are not helping them, they are failing them and you are misleading them, just tell them the truth.

Chapter Five

Just a Reminder Who Jesus Is

Revelation 1:8 KJV

8: I am Alpha and Omega, the beginning and the ending, saith the Lord which is, and which was, and which is to come, the Almighty.

Not only he's Jesus, he's Alpha and Omega, he's the beginning and he's the ending, he's peace, he's joy, he's love, he's faithful and he's the same God yesterday, today and forever more. Jesus can save you, Jesus can do anything because he's Alpha and Omega. Show me, anyone that can turn water into wine, show me anybody that can touch someone and bring back life there's only one man that can perform miracles. It's sickness all over the world and people are willing to stay in sin how can you trust someone on earth who has no power? You should be talking about the beginning and the ending which are Alpha and Omega, understand that life isn't the same when Jesus lays his hands on you remove flesh and come to Jesus remove your wicked nasty ways and come to Jesus he will fix it for you. I thank God that I don't carry the label of sin, you must come out of sin to get to your next place in life. You can cry out, you can reach out, God will hear your cry when you call for him, and God will reach out and take you in and do what he needs to do for you in holiness.

It's a new life it's a new path it's a new talk it's a new walk someone is crying out now fix it Jesus, I don't understand why people take living save for a joke you run in and out the church you run in needing God to do something and when God fix it you run back out the church but understand God doesn't need us we need him. This is why the devil don't want you to come out of sin and another reason why the devil don't want you to open your mouth because the devil know that it is power in Jesus and Jesus can do anything that you want him to do you just have to open your mouth and stand on the word of God and trusted in the Lord because Jesus doesn't fail us it's us that fail God you must live in the image of God so understand that you are not forced to go to hail it's up to you to choose life of death Jesus told us that he is the resurrection and the life and Jesus tells us that I am that I am so how can you use this saying for I am that I am to defeat the devil? Tell yourself that I am healed I am set free I am loved I am the fathers child and I am has giving me the power to live right and over come whatever life style isn't right we must live life by the blood of Jesus Christ, come now all God children for he went to the cross and paid the price for our sins God love you all just come to your first love which is Jesus Christ be healed by the blood be set free by the blood of Jesus. I don't care what the devil want you to believe it's all a lie when the devil speaks but when Jesus speaks you can take it to the bank because he said I shall never lie trust God and come out and be set free. I thank God that I over came the world and I live just for him to work in me I am pleased with my life I cry out to God everyday because I know if it wasn't for Jesus who was on my side the devil would have took be out but God wouldn't let it be so because he had a work for me to do and I'm doing what God has called me to do I walk in his anointing I am free from dry bones this is why I can tell the world that Jesus is your way in and your way out

You Are Not Born Thay Way

Praise his Holy Name for he is good. Walk in the anointing and see for yourself that Jesus will do what he says I love to hear from God because it blesses my soul it makes me stronger when I look back over my life it gives me joy on the inside because I made it out you can make it out as well just try Jesus and call on his Holy name don't allow anyone to keep you in that dry place move as God would have you to move we must let go of sin and hold on to Jesus because he is our first and our last love when it's all said and done one day you have to face Jesus you don't want to face him and he say I knew you not face Jesus now and give everything to him, leave the world and set over into Holiness. I know there are many people who have read my first book and I thank God for what he has done in their life and what he is yet to do understand that some of you that's living in sin God has a calling for you to do in this life and you must come out of sin and obey God you must come out and work for Jesus this is the only way you will find peace in your life running from Jesus won't give you peace it's when you come to him and give your life back to him put your life and his hand. Father God I ask that you bring your people bring them back to you were they will find love joy peace and long suffering Lord I ask that you send your blood to them that they may find you and your love in the name of Jesus do it Lord for only you can these thing I ask in your son Jesus Name Amen.

The Blood of Jesus is your weapon because living in sin, there is no life, but we are saved through the blood of Jesus. We are bought with the precious blood of Christ Jesus which is the pure Lamb, we don't plead for the blood anymore, and we don't worship the blood anymore, but we put everything else before the blood of Jesus. Sin has tried to make the blood sound foolish sin has tried to remove the blood from the world but what sin doesn't understand is the world belongs to the blood, but as for me in my house, we gone plead the blood of

Jesus because the blood shall never loose it's power. We have and must understand what the blood has already done and what the blood is about to do, I thank God because I have the blood of Jesus and I know the blood is about to save and set free the Holy Ghost's power. Blood is about to free some souls because God has called some of your names but you will not come to him but you must obey and use the weapon that God has sent to the world the blood of Jesus. Let this be a prayer for you to ask God to stretch out in you because the blood will make a difference in your life.

In the book of **Exodus KJV**, it tells us how the blood kept the children of Israel and also it tells us in Exodus that Jesus is the pass-over Lamb, sickness shall pass over pain, shall pass over death, shall pass over hurt, and shall pass over fear because the blood of Jesus is your weapon. Joshua said Jesus is the captain of my salvation, Ruth said Jesus is our Redeemer, Job said Jesus is our living Redeemer, David said Jesus is our Shephered, Jeremiah said Jesus is the righteous branch, Hosea said Jesus is the faithful Husband forever married to the backslider, Joel said Jesus is the baptizer of the Holy Ghost and firer. Jesus is everything you need, the blood is Jesus Christ. Take the blood and push away everything and everyone that's not of God push back to sin and be healed in Jesus name because the blood says that he will save and set free and deliver tell that devil that the blood said that you will be set free because with the blood hope is still alive and you can live again, so what do you want the blood to do for you?

Chapter Six

Bring it to Jesus

Bring your troubles to Jesus, and bring your sins to Jesus because Jesus is the problem solver. Cast all your cares upon the Lord, the devil is working harder now because the devil knows we are living in the last days, that's why I am saying to you in this book, bring all you have to Jesus, Jesus can and he will work it out for you. I know sometimes it gets hard, I know sometimes we fall weak, I know sometimes we feel like giving up and sometimes we ask if is it worth it, but I want to tell you to bring it all to Jesus. That husband or wife who wants to do right give them to Jesus, because God is a man who can do the impossible. Jesus is a man who understands he will never leave or forsake you. It's time to trust in the Lord, we trust everything and everyone else, but we will trust in Jesus. I dare you to cast your cares on him, allow Jesus to set you free in your heart and in your mind fall on your knees and cry out to him Jesus will break the yokes off your life Jesus has already paid the price for your sin. Don't ignore God because God will not ignore your call to him. God is the same God as he was back then. God has given you space and time to play out in the world long enough. Now it's time to repent and give it to Jesus, he will pour out on you to receive the power of the Holy Ghost because the Holy Ghost can only work in a clean temple. How much more time do you need and how much more time do you think we have? We are living in the last times, just look at what's going on in the world today and when the world has come to an end. It's two places, hell or heaven, ask yourself where would you go.

We must stop sinning and come to God. A lot of people know what they should be doing for God but they love sin more than they love Jesus, when Jesus is the reason you rise every morning. Sin isn't waking you up, it's by the grace of God that you are able to open your eyes every day because if it was up to the devil, you wouldn't be here because the devil's job is to kill, steal and destroy but the devil doesn't have power over our life. Jesus has all power, Jesus is Alpha and Omega, the one that has life and death in his hands. We must come out of the corrupt world and the corrupt churches and find that church home where the truth is coming forward teaching Holiness or Hell. Bring it all to Jesus so he can give you that spiritual birth. I love the saying Jesus is evidence the cross is evidence and we must face the truth. Jesus told Nicodemus, If tell you things that are plain as the hand before your face and you don't believe me, then Jesus asked what use is there in telling you of things you can't see, things of God. We must stay woke to the word of God, we can't stay blind to the truth. We have to be born again of water and of the Holy Spirit, everything that's on earth is evidence of Jesus.

So why is it that we act like we can't see the works of God, we can't see the spiritual things? I will tell you why because we are too caught up in worldly things. Our bodies are the evidence of Jesus this is why I temple should be clean when Jesus told the Jews to destroy this temple and I will raise it up in three days the Jews thought Jesus was talking about the building but Jesus was talking about the temple of his body, we must understand that Jesus is upright and clean, so that's what we should be upright and clean because we are the evidence of Jesus Christ.

God didn't send his son to condemn the world, but that the world through him may be saved. Come to Jesus and allow him to clean your temple, I told God I would do what it takes to get all that he had for me because sometimes it takes us putting things down and leaving things and people behind to get where we need to be in Jesus. This is another reason why I am telling you to bring it to Jesus so you can get what you need from him. Pray this prayer, with me Lord help me to stop doing things that you wouldn't do. Help me to stop thinking things that you wouldn't think help me to stay away from the things and people that are no good for me Lord. I bring it all to you because I know in my heart that you will bring me out and save me if I call upon your name. Help me to stand still and wait on you. Help me not to move until you say move but move on the inside of me when you see it. Jesus, help me to keep my eyes on you, for I know that you are the hope of Glory. Help me because I need you in my life as my Lord and savor these things. I ask in your son Jesus name Amen.

I want to encourage you to try Jesus and if you have Jesus, don't let go of him. Follow the path of Jesus and you will be blessed, see a lot of people just want the blessing, but I need the blesser because if I have the blesser and I am living right, all the other things will fall in place. Find you a prayer partner where the two of you can touch and agree in the name of Jesus. In **Matthew 18:20** says *For where two or three are gathered together in my name, there I am in the mix.* I am praying for you because I am praying for the world for people to be saved and do Gods will and I pray for everyone who touches this book that God will work in their life and bless save and set free God bless you all.

To My God Father Evangelist Robert L. Shepherd Jr., thank you for all the prayers that you have prayed for me. I thank God for you, thank you for being there for me when I needed someone to talk to. One of your books that you wrote titled "Surrender All to God or Be Deceived" made me look at life differently and I knew after reading this book, I had to give my all to God and I had to keep pushing toward Jesus and not looking back. Thank you God Father for being a true Father and friend, love you.

To my uncle and Pastor James Williams SR., thank you for being my leader and giving me the long talks when I need them and you the most, I know that you are praying for me and I thank God that we are able to do the will of God together. Not only are you a true man of God and uncle, you are a true friend, love you.

Shalamar Williams

www.ingramcontent.com/pod-product-compliance
Lightning Source LLC
LaVergne TN
LVHW050027080526
838202LV00069B/6952